ANTI

AN INTRODUCTION TO

RACIST

ACTION & ACTIVISM

ALLY

SOPHIE WILLIAMS

@OFFICIALMILLENNIALBLACK

An imprint of HarperCollinsPublishers Ltd
1 London Bridge Street, London SE1 9GF

This edition 2020

First published in Great Britain by HQ,
an imprint of HarperCollinsPublishers Ltd 2020

ISBN: 978-0007985128

Cover design and typesetting by Rebecca Petts Davies

MIX
Paper from
responsible sources
FSC™ C007454

Printed and bound in Great Britain by
Bell and Bain Ltd, Glasgow

ANTI RACIST ALLY

CONTENTS

INTRODUCTION

Hi! Congratulations on taking your first step in becoming an anti-racist ally. I'm so glad to have you here.

This book is deliberately small and a starting point for those who want to learn to become anti-racist allies, by joining the fight for racial equality, or for those who have already made a start but don't know what to do next, or how to keep up the momentum.

It's a bite-sized introduction to the things you need to know to lay the best foundation in your anti-racist allyship journey. You can share it with people in your life who want to use their voices and platforms to make the world a better place but don't know where to begin, or those with whom you want to have difficult conversations. It's a small and accessible resource for you to refer back to along the way.

Although I've spent years working in and talking about social justice, I began writing this book in the wake of the series of tragic murders that shocked the world in 2020 and galvanised many who had never considered their role in anti-racism to take action in their own lives.

I want to be honest with you from the very start, allyship is not always easy – there are no shortcuts or quick wins – but it's nowhere near as difficult as facing racism in your everyday life. You will have conversations with people who simply do not want to change the way things have always been. Speaking truth to power and saying it with your whole chest is not meant to be easy. If it were, it would have already happened. There will be a lot of times when you feel that you're pushing against a brick wall. There will be other times when it feels like you're making good progress, only to be told 'no' or be let down at the last minute. Moments like that can't be the end of your journey, they must instead be a chance to regroup, take stock and try again, even harder than before.

The purpose of this book is to challenge the things we've been taught based on white supremacy, and to seek better and fairer ways to move forward. Questioning the ways by which we operate can feel threatening, or even like an attack, and our response to that can be to close ourselves off and become defensive. It's important to remember that this is a learning process, and part of that is facing difficult truths, feeling uncomfortable and working through that. Fight the urge to pull away, and make space for discomfort.

Finally, while anti-racism is the focus of this book, the conversation about allyship is not limited to race. Each of us is an individual, made up of several facets. Our race is one of these, but so is our sexuality, gender identity, neurodiversity, class, socio-economic status, disability status, among many others. I hope some of the things we discuss here will help you to feel empowered and encouraged to be the best ally that you can be to all marginalised people.

We need you to be a part of the change.

DISCUSSION OF TERMS

I thought long and hard about the terms to use in this book about anti-racist allyship. I am a Black woman, and so my instinct is to focus on Blackness, as that is where the majority of my research and the entirety of my lived experience lies. However, we all know that Black people are not the only group marginalised due to the colour of our skin in Western society, so to exclude all other marginalised groups doesn't feel right.

On the other hand, I do not like the terms BIPOC, BAME or POC. That's right, I said it. The reason I don't like them is that I believe, despite these being terms used to refer to non-white people, every one of them centres on whiteness. BIPOC, BAME and POC all split people into just two groups – white and other.

In each case, whiteness is a group on its own, distinct from all else. Whiteness stands alone as the status quo against which all other ethnic groups are defined. Everyone who isn't white is lumped together through terms like BAME, POC and BIPOC without thought for their individual experiences. In this way white becomes a binary – white or not white – and all of the subtlety, richness and variety of different groups is whitewashed away.

After much internal deliberation I have decided to say 'marginalised groups' or just 'marginalised' so far as possible, rather than to use a term I find difficult, or to focus on Blackness at the expense of other marginalised racial groups. On occasions where, for one reason or another, this isn't possible, I will use BIPOC (Black, Indigenous, People of Colour – a term that puts those who are most impacted in that society front and centre) and BAME (Black, Asian, Ethnic Minority) as used by researchers whose work I'm referencing.

When I say 'society' I am speaking about Western society, and I appreciate that the nuances of race and racism are not universally similar.

I originally wrote this book with the spelling 'womxn' throughout in order to be inclusive. However, this spelling has since become a term co-opted by those who want to deny the true womanhood of trans and non-binary women. So instead I have used 'women', but please know that when I say women I mean all who identify as such, and that all women are real women.

1. NOT BEING RACIST IS NOT ENOUGH

'I'm not racist' is a good place to start, and I presume if you're reading this you're not a racist person, which is great. But I'm sorry to say, this really is the absolute bare minimum.

When people say they're not racist, they're usually thinking something along the lines of, 'I see everyone the same, and I would never discriminate against someone based on the colour of their skin'.

But what they're not thinking about is being actively anti-racist.

Not being racist is the right foundation, but it's a passive state. It's not allyship. To be an effective anti-racist ally, we all need to be actively anti-racist.

Sophie Williams

WHAT IS ANTI-RACISM?

Anti-racism is not about seeing and treating everyone in exactly the same way. Instead it's about understanding the different experiences, perspectives and (dis)advantages of people from different groups, and working to overcome them.

Anti-racism doesn't gloss over our differences or whitewash the experiences of others.

Anti-racism is about refusing to turn a blind eye when we see discrimination. It's about taking an active stance in our daily lives, calling out every joke, offhand comment, and act of injustice.

Anti-racism is not about self-improvement: being a better person is not the end goal. It's about creating a fairer society for marginalised people, which is a better world for us all.

Anti-racism, and working towards being an anti-racist ally, isn't easy, and it can be uncomfortable or even scary, but it's the only way we're going to make progress.

So let's get going.

Sophie Williams

RACISTS ARE BAD PEOPLE. I'M NOT A RACIST

The conversation around racism that most of us have heard since childhood is usually pretty one-dimensional.

Very black and white.

Racism is bad.

People who are racist are bad people.

And *you* are a good person, so you are not racist.

Since childhood we have been building up our personal mental images of 'a racist' – someone who is uncaring, violent, dangerous, hateful. You'd know one if you saw one and you'd definitely never be one.

But it doesn't quite work like that in practice.

Don't get me wrong, I'm not saying it's not true that racism is bad (I can't believe I just had to say that), but I'm also saying that the conversation is more nuanced than that simple good/bad binary leaves space for.

Instead of helping marginalised groups, this good/bad, black/white binary has made it really difficult for us to find the grey when we come to examine our own lives, actions and the systems that have benefited us along the way.

Sophie Williams

ISN'T RACISM OVER?

The reassuring thing about the idea of racist people being 80s skinheads or members of the KKK dressed in white robes is that they're easy to spot. If you find yourself burning a cross in a white hood one day, you might have accidentally become 'a racist'. If you beat up people from other races in the street or refuse to hire someone because of the colour of their skin then, uh oh, you got racist.

The reality is, that's just not what the majority of racist actions really look like in 2020.

Culture and society have both changed, and that means so have people's expectations and views of what is socially acceptable. In response, racism has had to find new, more coded and less overt ways to exist.

Being less overt doesn't mean it's less bad, it just means that it's more slippery, harder to identify, harder to report and harder to point to.

Modern racism is still dangerous, systemic and structural. It still kills people, takes away their rights, their dignity and their chance of having a fair shot at the lives we all deserve and that many take for granted.

Sophie Williams

I'M COLOUR-BLIND, I TREAT EVERYONE THE SAME

Maybe you're not actively anti-racist, but you're not racist. In fact, you'd go as far as to call yourself colour-blind. You treat everyone exactly the same, just like everyone else should.

When people claim 'colour-blindness' or that they treat everyone the same, it's usually from a place of good intentions. However, this is generally something people from marginalised ethnic groups don't say because they know that though individuals might strive for this, the reality is simply that society as a whole does not do this.

A one-size-fits-all, 'colour-blind', 'I treat everyone exactly the same way' approach overlooks an important factor: intersectionality. (See page 46 to learn more about intersectionality and why it matters.) Let's be honest with ourselves, structures were not built with equality for everyone in mind.

This means that, in practice, treating everyone the same leads less to equality and more to erasure, as we often leave the most marginalised people vulnerable to falling through the cracks.

A more inclusive approach is to recognise people's differences, to be good allies to them and to understand them as whole people.

Sophie Williams

I DON'T REALLY THINK ABOUT RACE VERY OFTEN

Going through life without thinking about, or being made aware of your race, is a privilege.

Marginalised people are aware of their race every day in a huge number of different ways.

- We have grown up with societal images of beauty that don't reflect us.

- We are reminded of our race by others when security guards follow us around shops for the crime of being a customer.

- We research places that we want to travel to, taking into consideration whether we will be safe and treated with respect.

- We are aware that if we call the police to protect us, we risk putting ourselves in more danger.

Sophie Williams

I CAN'T BE RACIST. MY WIFE/ HUSBAND/ BOSS/ BEST FRIEND/ DENTIST IS BLACK

'I can't be racist because this or that person I know is Black' is something I've heard time and time again.

Let me be clear here: your proximity to non-whiteness does not give you a free pass.

It never has, and it never will.

People from marginalised backgrounds are not accessories that can be used or pointed at 'prove' your anti-racism. We understand that misogynists date and marry women, and have other women in their lives who they care about, maybe even love and respect. This doesn't mean they're not misogynistic.

The same is true for racism.

You can have marginalised people who are close in your life and still be racist.

The only thing that can show your anti-racism is the active anti-racism work that you do and the stands that you take.

2. BECOME AN ANTI-RACIST ALLY

Not being racist isn't allyship.

But being actively anti-racist, fighting for a cause that you really believe in?

That's more like it.

Be an anti-racist ally.

Sophie Williams

ALLIES VS WHITE SAVIOURS

To break it down into its simplest possible terms:
being an ally is good, being a white saviour is not.

But what's the difference?

White saviours are not what we're looking for, because
rather than listening to, respecting and being led by the
voices of marginalised people and communities, they
instead put themselves at the centre of the issue and, as a
result, dehumanise those who they are claiming to help.
An easy example of this is people who post pictures of
themselves on social media surrounded by Black faces at
an orphanage they taught at or helped to build or visited
last summer. They are smiling among a sea of Black children, signalling to their online audience that they are,
indisputably, a good person.

The bodies of marginalised people become props in the
furthering of the Look How Well I'm Doing narrative of
the saviour.

In examples like this, those people can be accused of using
those images, those people's bodies and their struggles to
signal their own virtuousness.

These one-off actions might be helpful, to an extent, if
researched and approached well and carefully. But they're
not allyship, and they often lack the research and investment to make them impactful and meaningful.

Sophie Williams

WHAT IS ALLYSHIP?

Allyship is what you do, not what you believe.

Allyship is speaking up, standing up; it's joining the fight and struggle to achieve equality for all.

Allyship leads from behind. It's not making it all about you or looking for praise or credit for your work, especially from marginalised people, but about listening to voices that too often go unheard and seeking to uplift and amplify them and their messages.

As an ally, your job is to make change.

Your job is to push past comfort and politeness and challenge the structures and norms that we've all grown up taking for granted, and be a part of creating the society you want to live in.

Even when it's difficult.

Especially when it's difficult.

It's still easier than facing racism and discrimination on a daily basis.

Allyship is not just fighting for those people you know or to whom you feel a connection, but for everyone, simply because it's the right thing to do.

Sophie Williams

BEING SHOCKED IS NOT ALLYSHIP

Being shocked is not allyship.

Saying, 'I can't believe it' is not allyship.

Feeling sympathy is not allyship.

Thinking that *someone* should do something is not allyship.

Taking on these issues as your own and fighting for them consistently, consciously, is allyship.

Feeling the injustice on your skin and in your stomach – and then turning those feelings into actions for the benefit of others. That's allyship.

Sophie Williams

UNDERSTAND HOW WHITE SUPREMACY HAS BENEFITTED YOU

White supremacy isn't just having extreme views on race, it's the privilege of being born with a skin colour that doesn't suffer at the hands of society's prejudice.

It's easy to not think too deeply about the culture we live in, what it's based on, who created it, or who benefits most from it. The way things are seems like the way they have always been, and should be – the status quo.

If we're comfortable with saying that society, as it is currently, disadvantages people who aren't white, then we have to take a moment to acknowledge the flip side of that, which is that society actively advantages people with white skin.That can be a hard thing for white people to come to terms with, because being white is so often seen as being raceless.

Western culture was built (not literally by, because we know who was really doing the lifting, carrying and building) to protect the privilege and rights of white people, and to ensure their children enjoyed these too.

Ways in which white people have benefited from white supremacist society include:

• Not being expected to speak for or represent your entire race.

• Not having to justify or debate your right to a safe and equal life.

• Being less likely to be stopped and questioned, searched or arrested by the police in day-to-day life.

Sophie Williams

ALLYSHIP IS HAVING DIFFICULT CONVERSATIONS

Allyship is having difficult conversations, exactly the ones we've been taught are rude and that we should avoid at all costs.

Death, sex, money, politics – all of these topics are impacted by race, and so they are also all areas that we need to get comfortable learning, thinking and talking about in order to be effective allies.

It's important to learn to accept and sit with the feeling of discomfort. Avoiding that feeling, prioritising comfort, means we avoid addressing the very things that need to be brought to light the most.

Sophie Williams

ALLYSHIP IS LONG-TERM

People who are newly engaged in civil rights and racial justice can be real driving forces, bringing renewed energy and passion to those who have been doing this work for much longer.

One risk for new allies, however, is becoming disheartened or frustrated with the pace of change. Change in this area has been slow – not weeks or months slow – more like decades and generations slow.

Geographic time.

Glacial speeds.

My fear as the headlines move on is that allies will too. Maybe we'll be back to square one. Or maybe we'll go further back than when we started if people begin to feel satisfied or resigned that they did their best to support the fight.

Marginalised groups have been fighting the same fights, having the same conversations, battling the same struggles that our parents and grandparents did. Most of us started doing this work knowing that our ancestors didn't live to see the impact of their struggles or make the changes they needed, and yet, we have had to persist.

You must also persist.

Allyship is for the long term. There are no quick fixes.

Sophie Williams

ALLYSHIP IS GLOBAL AND LOCAL

It's important to be aware of the global context of racism if we're going to be able to identify where the biggest challenges lie, and when the wins happen.

Take time to educate yourself on the issues and injustices around the world to understand the bigger picture and truly grasp how marginalised people are discriminated against, and how allyship can transcend borders.

Once you've got the global picture, it's time to think locally about the changes you can make at home.

Most people's strongest sphere of influence is with the people closest to them.

Finding ways to make positive change in the opinions or actions of people and organisations closest to you can be a good way of maximising success, from changing policies in schools to having an impact on local government.

It also gives us a chance to see in real time the impact of your work, which can be rewarding and motivating.

See pages 134 – 47 to become an ally at home and in your communities.

Sophie Williams

ALLYSHIP IS HOLDING SPACE, NOT TAKING IT UP

Holding space is something we ask allies to do, while taking up space is something allies must avoid. But what do we really mean and what's the difference?

Taking up space is re-centring the conversation around yourself. It's taking away space, oxygen and attention from the voices of the same marginalised people who we claim to be supporting.

Holding space means listening without judgement, and accepting the truth of someone else's experiences as they tell them.

Holding space is understanding the privilege that means you can access spaces and platforms that marginalised people can't, and using your voice once you're in those spaces to elevate and amplify those who are kept outside.

Sophie Williams

ALLYSHIP IS INTER-SECTIONAL

Anti-racist allyship doesn't mean picking and choosing which Black, brown or marginalised lives matter.

We don't get to exclude people on the basis of their gender, religion, sexuality, gender identity, class, lifestyle or anything else.

We don't get to prioritise light-skinned, or 'well-spoken', or other 'socially acceptable' marginalised people.

The more marginalised identities people have, the more they need the support of their communities and allies, not less.

3.
LET'S TALK ABOUT INTERSECTIONALITY

'There is no such thing as a single-issue struggle, because we do not live single-issue lives' – Audre Lorde.

We are all made up of a range of complex identities. Understanding a person, their life and their challenges means understanding them in their wholeness, and supporting all elements of them, not just the ones we find easiest to relate to.

Sophie Williams

WHAT IS INTERSEC- TIONALITY?

We are all made up of a number of facets, such as our race, gender identity, sexuality, disabilities, neurological diversities, class, skin tone and many others.

Intersectionality is a term coined by Black feminist and thinker Kimberlé Crenshaw in 1989, which recognises that disadvantaged identities don't cancel each other out, instead they layer on top of each other, creating overlapping, heightened, experiences of discrimination.

Intersectionality recognises these overlaps, and understands that due to these intersections, not all marginalised experiences are the same, as some face double, triple, or even more layers of societal disadvantage.

Sophie Williams

WHY DOES INTERSEC- TIONALITY MATTER?

We never interact with only one element of a person, and neither does society.

Instead we interact with individuals as whole people, and so we need to understand them in those terms.

The issues that impact an able-bodied Black woman are not identical to those that impact a disabled Black woman.

A cisgender Indian man has a different lived experience to a non-binary counterpart.

We must recognise intersectional identities, rather than grouping all marginalised people into the same box of 'otherness' if we are to be effective allies.

Sophie Williams

INTERSEC-TIONALITY & ALLYSHIP

Being an ally is not about picking a narrow subset of people who fit easily into our world view and our beliefs, then uplifting them. For example, when we say Black Lives Matter we must mean *all* Black lives, including and especially the most disadvantaged within this group.

To be good and effective allies we must recognise these intersectional advantages and disadvantages and how we can best help the most marginalised people in our society. When we fail to do so, we don't give the correct support to those who need it the most.

Sophie Williams

YOU CAN BE OPPRESSED AND THE OPPRESSOR AT THE SAME TIME

Just because you are oppressed in one area of your life doesn't mean that you can't be an oppressor in another, even unintentionally.

Think about the privileges that you have and how you can best use those to be an effective ally, even if you too have experienced oppressions in other areas of your life.

4.
WHAT DOES RACISM LOOK LIKE NOW?

If we're going to be anti-racist allies, we should know what we're fighting against.

Racism as an issue is huge. Without real, tangible examples of what it looks like and how it manifests today, we don't stand a good chance of winning the fight against it.

So, what does racism look like now?

Overall, modern-day racism is less black face and racial slurs and more insidious, coded and systemic discrimination. This nonetheless costs people their lives and chips away at their physical and mental health, wellbeing, wealth and security day by day. So it's vital that we can recognise just a few of the ways it presents itself.

You should never ask marginalised people to provide you with all the answers to things you can find out for yourself. But, just this once, I'm going to break this rule and share some basic answers to common questions around racism today. This is by no means an exhaustive list.

I'm doing this so your friends don't have to.

Sophie Williams

WHAT IS INTER- PERSONAL RACISM?

Interpersonal racism is racism between individuals, or groups of people, based on personally held racist beliefs and stereotypes.

Interpersonal racism can be verbal, physical, or psychological, and it is the most common type of racism that we think about.

When I was a child I got pushed into my primary school gates, called a racial slur, and punched in the face. That is interpersonal racism.

Street harassment, workplace bullying and microaggressions are all examples of interpersonal racism.

Sophie Williams

WHAT ARE INSTITUTIONAL AND STRUCTURAL RACISM?

Institutional racism is the way in which institutions and organisations uphold and continue racism that discriminates against marginalised people. This could be in the ways that banks lend money, how schools enforce discipline, how businesses pay their staff, and even who they hire.

If two people are doing the same job, with the same outputs, in the same business as one another, but one of them receives a lower salary because they're from a marginalised ethnic group, that's institutional racism.

Structural racism is interpersonal and institutional racism combined, in larger structures, such as the government and law making. This could be in the ways that criminal justice is practised, how the police make decisions about stop and search, how council or community housing is segregated and who has access to healthcare providers.

Black people in the UK are 40 times more likely to be stopped and searched by the police than white people.[1] That is structural racism.

Sophie Williams

WHAT IS THE RACE PAY GAP?

The race pay gap is intersectional disadvantage in action. We often talk about the gender pay gap, something that large businesses are required in many countries to be transparent about in their annual reporting of salaries.

We often hear that if the gender pay gap continues to close at the rate that it is currently, white women will achieve pay parity by 2059. What we talk about less often is that when we separate out a single group, like Black women, that story becomes worse. Black women will have to work until 2130 to close the race and gender pay gap.[2]

In the US, for every dollar that a white man earns, a Black woman earns an average of just 61 cents. According to the National Women's Law Centre, over a 40-year career that creates a loss of $946,120. To put it another way, to close the gap that's created by nothing more than the double disadvantages of being Black and female, a Black woman in America would need to work until she was 86 to accumulate the same earnings as a white man who retired at 60.[3]

When we don't consider race, we only tell half of the story.

Not receiving equal pay for equal work is racism and misogyny combined.

Sophie Williams

WHAT IS OCCUPATIONAL SEGREGATION?

Occupational segregation is a term usually used to discuss gender differences in industries or occupations. What's usually left out of this conversation is racial occupational segregation: the inability of non-white people to access well-paid jobs and secure roles across industries due to biased hiring and recruitment practices.

This lack of access means that even if we were able to close the pay gap for people doing the same roles, there would still be both a gender and race pay gap because occupational segregation limits marginalised groups' ability to access well-paying, secure roles.

In the UK, young Black people are the group most likely to be employed on insecure, often under-regulated, zero-hours contracts, and are more likely to have a second job in order to make ends meet.[4]

In the US, because they are more likely to be clustered in roles and industries that are perceived as low status, and which command lower pay, workers from marginalised racial backgrounds are much more likely to be in jobs that pay poverty level wages than white workers – hourly wages that would leave them and their families below the federal poverty line, even if they work full-time.

In 2017, 8.6 per cent of white workers were paid poverty wages, compared to 19.2 per cent – nearly one in five – of Hispanic workers and 14.3 per cent of Black workers.[5]

Sophie Williams

WHAT IS EMOTIONAL LABOUR?

Emotional labour is the unpaid, often invisible work that's put on the shoulders on marginalised people when they are asked or expected to be the unofficial teachers, pathfinders and emotional support crutches of other people.

Asking marginalised friends to rehash their most traumatic experiences for your learning is emotional labour.

Asking marginalised people to validate you in your non-racism, is emotional labour.

Asking marginalised people to explain, debate or justify why their lives matter while you 'play' devil's advocate is emotional labour.

While this work may seem trivial, it's deeply emotionally draining, and it has damaging effects on the lives and mental and physical health of already marginalised groups.

Before reaching out in these ways, ask if this is the best use of someone's limited time, if this is work you'd be happy to be asked to take on for free, and if this is work or education you could take on for yourself.

Learning is great, but putting someone else in the position of having to teach you is not.

Sophie Williams

WHAT IS TONE POLICING?

Tone policing is a tactic used to silence people whose thoughts and experiences others would rather not hear.

Instead of engaging with what someone has said, tone policing instead addresses and attacks the tone with which it is said in order to discredit the speaker without having to engage with their points.

This is common time and time again in race discussions. It limits the range of emotions marginalised people are allowed to express if they want to be taken seriously, and diminishes their personhood.

Some examples of tone policing are:

'If you weren't so emotional maybe you'd get a better result.'

'Well, maybe if you just said it more nicely...'

'Why don't you calm down, then we can talk about this.'

Sophie Williams

WHAT IS RED-LINING?

Redlining was the practice in the 1930s of the literal drawing of red lines on maps around 'undesirable' areas, in order to determine good and bad parts of cities and towns.

While this was most prevalent in the US, it was by no means the only country to use it.

These classifications were not based on the income or economic strength of the people in these areas, but on the area's racial makeup.

'Good' areas were mainly white, and 'bad' areas were mainly not.

These classifications in turn determined where banks were located, where they would make mortgage loans, and to whom.

'Bad' areas received less investment in public services such as healthcare and public transport, and attracted fewer desirable business such as supermarkets, resulting in the creation of food deserts.

Redlining made sure that racially diverse areas become poorer and the people living in them remained under-served disadvantaged.

Sophie Williams

WHAT IS THE SCHOOL-TO-PRISON PIPELINE?

From the very beginning of their time at school, racially marginalised children have a different experience to that of their white peers.

Marginalised children, and particularly Black children, are perceived as being older and less innocent than white children of the same age.[6] With prejudiced views such as these, combined with zero-tolerance attitudes to bad behaviour means it's no wonder that Black and brown pupils are over-represented in school exclusions and Pupil Referral Centres.[7]

When a marginalised student is expelled from a school, all too often that marks the end of their contact with the schooling system as a whole, and the beginning of increased contact with the criminal justice system.

Sophie Williams

WHAT IS RACIAL GASLIGHT- ING?

Racial gaslighting is diminishing the lived experiences of marginalised people, usually by suggesting that they're 'overreacting', 'making a fuss', or 'can't take a joke'.

Racial gaslighting can also be tone policing, victim blaming, questioning a person's truth when they say they have been the victim of racism, or simply denying the existence of racism outright.

Being constantly disbelieved, told we're making things up, or having people who make racist comments towards us explain why we're wrong and they were, in fact, not being racist, and it's *us* who is the problem, chips away at the daily lives of marginalised groups.

Saying we are overreacting or inventing issues casts us as unreliable narrators of our own lived experiences.

Sophie Williams

WHAT IS COLOURISM?

Proximity to whiteness is a privilege, even if you're not a white person. As a very light-skinned Black woman, this is something I know first hand.

Let me explain.

Look at the marginalised people who are cast to play main roles on TV shows, or used in adverts to sell products. Look at those who are shown on the front covers of magazines, or even those who progress to hold positions of high political office, they're usually pretty light-skinned.

Another way to say this is that they have a high proximity to whiteness: they're not white, but they're often not that dark either.

We give advantages to those close enough to whiteness to be seen as non-threatening, but still dark enough that brands, editors, voters are able to self-congratulate on their diversity efforts while continuing to prioritise the whitest version of non-whiteness.

When we are fighting for anti-racism, we are not just fighting for the lives of those with high proximity to whiteness, but for all marginalised people, from the very lightest to the very darkest, and everyone in between.

5.
ALLYSHIP
ANXIETIES

People delay starting their allyship journeys for a number of reasons. The silent end to the sentence 'I didn't know where to start' is too often 'so I didn't do anything'.

Often times, people see or hear something that they know to be wrong, but don't want to take the risk of getting involved, ruffling feathers or inserting themselves into conversations that are 'none of their business'.

Here are some common allyship anxieties, and how to overcome them.

Sophie Williams

I DON'T KNOW WHERE TO START

Well, this one is nice and easy, because you already have!

Taking the first step to allyship can be intimidating. We can feel frozen in place by the fear of getting it wrong or the sheer size of the task ahead of us.

If you're reading this, if you're thinking about your role as an anti-racist ally, you've already made a start.

Sophie Williams

THIS ISN'T MY FIGHT

The fight for justice and equality is everyone's fight.

Marginalised people are exactly that: marginalised.

We are overlooked, not listened to, treated as less important than our white counterparts. For a long time, marginalised people were literally disenfranchised, and in a lot of ways, many still are.

We have been fighting this fight, with our hearts and souls, since before we can remember. We have been putting our bodies directly into harm's way in the hope that even if we don't live to see change, we can be a part of making it.

The systems of oppression were not made by us, and they cannot be dismantled by us alone.

This must be a team effort.

There must be allies.

Sophie Williams

I DON'T WANT TO MAKE THIS ALL ABOUT ME

This is a really good worry to have.

Not wanting to make it all about you is a great thing to keep in mind as you practise anti-racist allyship, and can be a guard rail against veering into the white saviour complex.

Make sure that you are listening to, learning from and amplifying the voices of those less privileged than you.

Take their lead, learn the language and credit your sources and you should be on a good and right path.

Sophie Williams

I DON'T HAVE ENOUGH OF A VOICE TO MAKE CHANGE

However small you think your voice or platform is, I promise you it can reach places that many marginalised voices can't.

When I made my first anti-racism posts and shared them online I had just a few hundred followers. I put up an imperfect post with typos, and a whole duplicated slide that makes me cringe every time I think about it. I never imagined that it would really be seen by anyone, let alone lead to all of this! The speed and volume of the response have shown me that however small we think our voices are, there are always people listening.

You have the power to change hearts and minds, particularly of those closest to you. Use that power.

Use your voice.

Stand tall in your convictions.

Say it with your whole chest.

You are more powerful than you know.

Sophie Williams

I DON'T WANT TO ALIENATE MY COMMUNITY

If your community is very closed, or close-knit, if it's putting marginalised people at a disadvantage or even at risk, then challenging ideas in it is a necessary wake-up call.

Closed communities with singular ways of thinking and points of view can be almost impossible for outsiders to communicate effectively with, and enable change in long-term.

The most effective forces for change in these groups can be allies who can bridge the gap in understanding and challenge unconscious biases.

Think of it as an undercover mission.

Ruffle some feathers.

Make necessary changes from the inside.

Sophie Williams

I FEEL LIKE IT'S NOT THE RIGHT TIME

There will never be a perfect time to start a difficult conversation. You can't wait for the opportunity, you have to *make* the opportunity.

It's incredibly rare to be handed the perfect, easy, safe moment to make a change. Instead, most of the time we have to make these moments ourselves in clunky, awkward, imperfect ways.

And even then, not only do you have to keep pushing, you then have to continue to look for ways by which you can make more opportunities for more people.

Taking our first stand can be nerve-wracking, without question. I know that when I started posting and talking about this topic, I felt exposed and under-prepared because I was. But the more we do it, the easier it will become. It will also enable others to follow our example.

Sophie Williams

I FEEL GUILTY

Sometimes feelings of guilt or shame about past beliefs or behaviours can hold us back from making positive change in our future.

Feeling guilty is fine, it shows you that you and your beliefs have grown, and it gives you an insight into the mindset of people who most need to hear the message of change.

If you feel guilty about your privilege, look for ways to now use that privilege for good.

If you feel guilty about things you've said or done in the past, look for ways to make reparations without centring your transformation in the process.

Use the knowledge that you have been capable of change to push for even greater development in yourself and those around you, rather than letting guilt or shame stop your potential for future change.

Sophie Williams

RACISM WILL DIE OUT IN A GENERA-TION

This is something I hear a lot.

So did my mom.

And my grandma.

It's not true.

Every generation points to the next as the saviours who will solve the issues they don't want to tackle head-on themselves.

Although it's true that no one is born racist, racism is taught, in subtle ways, from the very beginning of children's lives. White children will have hardships, but their race will almost certainly not be one of them.

Non-white children will have joys, but they will also still be growing up in societies where they are marginalised.

Until the structural issues on which our societies are built are addressed, racism will continue to be a life and death issue.

Sophie Williams

I DON'T WANT TO MAKE A MISTAKE

You will make mistakes. You will get things wrong, even things that you do when you're 100 per cent sure that you're right.

I know. I've been there.

You can't let a desire to be perfect overpower a chance to do good.

Remember, you are learning.

If it's a choice between making a mistake and doing nothing, make the mistake.

Learn from it.

Keep doing the work.

Say sorry.

Keep it moving.

Don't make the same mistake twice.

6.
START WITH YOURSELF

When we become aware of injustices in the world, it can be our first instinct to jump in head first and try to make change.

Before we can make a real impact on the world around us, it's important that we start by educating and questioning ourselves.

Prioritise learning. There is a long and rich history of anti-racist activism that we are building on.

Take time to learn from historical and contemporary leaders in this field, in order to build on the foundations that they have laid.

See page 174 to find suggestions for further reading.

Sophie Williams

BREAK YOUR ECHO CHAM- BER

It's easy and comfortable to spend time with and talk to people who share our ideas and ideals about the world around us.

These echo chambers amplify the messages that we already hear, and give us the false impression that everyone, or at least everyone we know, believes the same things as us.

The agreement of others echoes back and crystalises our own ideas, making it hard for us to hear and take on other challenging ideas and perspectives.

It's important to put ourselves in positions where we can hear a range of different views. Don't fall into the trap of feeling that the work is done and the fight is won just because you only hear the thoughts of like-minded people.

It's crucial to engage with and challenge views that don't align with our own. Those who don't agree with us are the ones that need to hear our message the most.

Sophie Williams

DIVERSIFY YOUR SOCIAL MEDIA

Most of us spend a lot of time on, and get a lot of information from social media.

Even if we don't consciously think of our social feed as a learning tool, it's normal that we absorb information presented to us by the people we choose to follow.

It's important to be mindful of who you follow.

Scroll through your feeds. Are you mostly following people who look similar to one another, and to yourself? Have they had similar lived experiences to one another, and you?

Following a limited range of people is easy to do, and most of the time we don't even know we're doing it.

Make an effort to seek out and engage with voices and experiences different to your own.

Be aware when diversifying your social feeds that individual people cannot be diverse. Collective things can be diverse – so you can build a diverse team at work, or follow a diverse range of people online – but a single person alone cannot be diverse. Labelling individuals as 'diverse' is othering, and only serves to single out the person you're referring to.

Sophie Williams

DON'T BLOCK YOUR RACIST 'FRIENDS'

There will be people on your social media, even people who you know, or have known at some point in your life, who will challenge or even troll us online in discussions of anti-racism.

It's natural to want to try to reason with these people, and get dragged into a series of back and forth comments on an increasingly uncomfortable public thread, before giving up and unfriending or blocking them.

I mean, after all, who needs 'friends' like that?

In moments like this, remember that opting out is a privilege, and one that people with different, darker, skin colours don't have.

Remember that people are more likely to have their hearts and minds changed by people who they know, and who they see elements of themselves in than by strangers.

Sophie Williams

TAKE TIME TO LISTEN

Take the time to really listen to marginalised people and their experiences, both good and bad.

When I say listen I don't just mean to hear, I mean really really listen.

I recommend having a period of listening without asking questions in the first instance. Many people find this difficult, but allowing yourself to observe and absorb before trying to reframe can be extremely valuable.

An important part of an ally's role is to amplify the voices of those who too often go unheard, but before that's possible it's essential to take the time to listen, understand and digest the things they want you to hear.

Sophie Williams

UNDERSTAND WHITE PRIVILEGE

White privilege, or majority privilege, is not saying that your life has been easy. But what it is saying is that whiteness, in many societies, is a privilege in itself.

White privilege doesn't wipe away individuals' challenges and difficulties in life, but what it does say is that race isn't one of those struggles.

We all face hurdles and obstacles in life, but for marginalised people those day-to-day challenges, such as job hunting, career progression, dating, or even feeling safe in your own space, have race as an additional layer of consideration and difficulty.

Sophie Williams

WHAT IS WHITE COMFORT?

White comfort describes the way in which all other groups alter their actions to make sure white people not feel uncomfortable or attacked.

As marginalised people, we know that if we talk candidly, openly, honestly about our feelings, fears and experiences we will be faced not only with disbelief, but also denial and hostility from many.

We have to edit the telling of our lives, dampen our feelings and tie our tongues in knots to make sure that we're expressing things in the most palatable way, going to great pains to be clear that it's not *you* we're talking about, we know *you* would never do such a thing.

In these ways, and in thousands of others, marginalised people perform invisible, daily labour to coddle, shield and protect white comfort at the expense of the rest of us being unable to express authentic experiences.

7.
BECOME AN ALLY IN YOUR SOCIAL CIRCLE

Becoming an ally in your social circle means two things:

1. Listening to the experiences of your marginalised friends, holding space for their feelings and using your voice and actions to fight on their behalf.

2. Engaging with your white friends, sharing the things you have learned, leading by example, and pushing them to be better allies themselves.

Our social circles are real opportunities for dialogue, collaboration and making quick and impactful change.

Sophie Williams

WHAT DOES YOUR SOCIAL CIRCLE LOOK LIKE?

If we're going to talk about allyship in our social circles, the first thing we need to do is take a good look at exactly who our friends are.

Can you honestly say that you have a diverse group of friends? If not, why is that?

If your friendship circle is diverse, are you someone with whom your non-white friends can be comfortable talking openly about their lived experiences? If not, why might that be?

Don't try to make new friends just because of the colour of their skin – this is tokenism and can be belittling to them as people. (Honestly, we know when we're your token Black friend.)

Instead, simply notice where you're starting from, and be conscious of the changes that happen as you continue in your public allyship.

Sophie Williams

LET YOUR ACTIONS SPEAK FOR THEMSELVES

Don't go out of your way to tell your friends that you are now an anti-racist ally. Instead do the work, consistently, and let your actions speak for themselves.

There will be people who don't like, or don't see the value in what you're doing. It's down to you whether you try to convince them, or focus your energy on areas where you can make clear change.

There will be many others who want to learn from your example, some will reach out to tell you, and others you will impact without ever knowing you did so.

The things you do and the actions you take have ripples that will spread far beyond you.

Sophie Williams

BUILD A SUPPORT SYSTEM

To be successful in your allyship it's important you have a support network and that you're conscious of other people's experiences and boundaries.

When you see photos, videos or articles about the injustices suffered by marginalised people on your news feeds, on TV or in the headlines, you might feel compelled to share it with non-white friends with a message of shock and disgust, and how sorry you are. I understand why you want to do this, but pay close attention when I say this: Please never do that again. It's vital not to re-traumatise your marginalised friends.

We share images of Black and brown bodies being beaten, dying, gasping for breath in ways that we would never dream of sharing images of white people. If your friend hasn't seen that particular piece, they will have seen countless others like it. We already know. We are living it.

So, who can you reach out to?

Reach out to your white friends, these are the people who need to hear the message the most, and those who are most likely to have the emotional capacity to give the support that you need.

Form a support system.

Keep each other on track and motivated.

Sophie Williams

HOLD SPACE FOR BLACK JOY

Working and fighting for change can be hard. It's draining work. Not least because when we begin, we are often bombarded by information about and images of Black and brown bodies suffering and in pain.

As well as having difficult conversations, make sure you are also holding space for Black and brown people to exist in your life as real, fully rounded, joyful people.

Read books about Black and brown people living, not just dying. Engage in content where they thrive, rather than just survive.

Remembering the full and complex range of lives and emotions in marginalised people is humanising, and a lot of fun.

You'll feel better for it.

Sophie Williams

BEWARE OF PERFORMATIVE ALLYSHIP

Now is not the time to start posting pictures of yourself next to every racially marginalised person you've ever met or had a drink with to prove that not only are you an ally, you always have been.

Again, being an ally isn't about proving to the world what a good person you are, but about fighting injustice and making long-term change.

Before you post a picture or even act, take a moment to consider: would you still be doing this if no one saw it?

If not, your allyship is performative, self-serving and unlikely to still be important to you once news cycles move on and Black Lives Matter stops trending.

8. BECOME AN ALLY IN YOUR WORKPLACE

Many of us spend a lot of our time at work. The workplace is an area where we can use our voices and our privileges to make positive, anti-racist differences.

Whether it's recruitment, retention, pay parity or promotions, once we start to examine the structures in which we work, we can start to identify inequalities, and push for real change.

Sophie Williams

TALK ABOUT YOUR PAY

Most of us have been told for as long as we can remember that talking about money is rude and should be avoided.

Many employers suggest that discussing salaries is not only frowned upon, but prohibited. So much so, that many people are under the false impressions that it is a sackable offence.

I want to be clear: not only is talking about money absolutely allowed, it's legally protected, and beneficial for everyone. Particularly marginalised people.

The race and gender pay gaps, as well as pay gaps for those with physical and neurological differences, mean that many people who are already from marginalised backgrounds continue to be underpaid and disadvantaged.

Talk openly about what you earn with people, particularly those in the same industry as you. We'll never spot the gaps that need to be filled by keeping the information in the dark.

Sophie Williams

BECOME A SPONSOR OR MENTOR

Workplace mentors and sponsors can make a huge difference to people's progression and happiness in the workplace.

Knowing that there is someone in a business who has your best interests at heart, who will advocate for you and help you to navigate difficult situations or opaque processes can change everything.

If you're in a position where you can reach out and offer someone regular support and guidance, where you can put them forward for training, an award or a promotion, do so. These small acts can change everything for someone who is struggling to find their way, particularly in industries with an Old Boys' Club mentality.

If you're not in a senior position, don't underestimate the power of horizontal mentorship. Reaching out to someone at the same level as you can make a difference in turning a hostile working environment into a more friendly one. Work with them to identify ways that together you can be more effective agents for necessary change.

Sophie Williams

DON'T LEAVE THE COMMITTEES TO THE MARGINALISED

When I think about how diversity and inclusion committees are run in many businesses, including many I've worked for personally, I want to scream. I can't tell you the number of times I've been told that they love what I stand for, and would I be willing to either be a part of their existing D&I committee, or set one up?

All too often these committees and task forces are not treated as a core part of a business. They are usually run by marginalised team members, juggling them on top of their existing work. This type of work is known as 'office housework', tasks that keep people busy, but are essentially invisible.

The opposite to office housework is 'glamour work'. This is the high-profile work, usually linked to bringing in revenue, which shines a positive light on the people who have the opportunity to take it on.

When people are overloaded with office housework on top of their day jobs, their capacity to take on glamour work is reduced. This means that not only are these extra tasks being siloed to one group of people, they take away the time that they could be focusing on more high-profile work that puts them in line for pay rises and promotions.

Don't leave office housework to marginalised people. Join your diversity and inclusion committee at work and fight for change on behalf of others.

Sophie Williams

A PROMISE IS NOT ENOUGH

It's easy for businesses to make flimsy, opaque promises about 'being more diverse' and 'making a change'.

'We want to be a more inclusive workplace' means nothing at all.

'We promise to be a more inclusive workplace' is slightly better.

'We promise to increase representation or marginalised groups, at management level and above, by 20 per cent in the next twelve months. We are also implementing a zero-tolerance policy of bullying and harassment, and introducing compulsory anti-bias training' is what we're looking for.

Push your employer to make time-based, measurable goals, to assign the necessary budgets to make them possible, and then hold them to account.

Recruitment, too, is a first step, not the end goal.

Hiring marginalised people into businesses where they might feel isolated, tokenised, where they will most likely be underpaid and promoted at a worse rate than their majority counterparts is not a recipe for happiness, or long-term retention.

Talk to your employer about what they can do to look beyond hiring to ensure their workplace is not only diverse, but inclusive.

Sophie Williams

STOP ASKING MARGINALISED PEOPLE TO WORK FOR FREE

People from marginalised backgrounds deserve to be paid for their time.

It sounds obvious, but I can't tell you the number of times well-intentioned people have reached out to ask me to do this or that part of their jobs for them, out of the goodness of my heart.

Asking knowledgeable people to help you in looking for ways to diversify your workplace, or to create an inclusive and welcoming space is fantastic – but only if you have the budget to compensate them for their time and efforts.

Don't expect marginalised people to take on work for free that others would be paid for. In a world where marginalised people already suffer from the wage gap, this is not allyship, it's exploitation.

9. BECOME AN AN ALLY AT HOME AND IN YOUR COMMUNITIES

Our life at home and the communities we're a part of are spheres where we have the most potential for real, impactful change.

Families have a much greater chance of changing each other's minds and impacting actions than people we don't know.

Communities, unless built carefully and conscientiously from the ground up, will reflect and mirror the societies in which they're built, which means they centre around whiteness, even if it's subconsciously.

This is an area where you have the potential to make real change, real impact, even if it feels uncomfortable or daunting at first.

Sophie Williams

RACISM IS NOT FOR CHILDREN

When we say racism isn't a topic for and doesn't affect children, what we really mean is racism isn't a topic for white children, because white children are (largely) unaffected by it.

This is a privilege that marginalised people do not have, because society treats marginalised children differently from the very start of their lives. In fact, many marginalised children experience the impact of medical bias and racism even before the start of their lives. Black mothers are five times more likely, and Asian mothers are twice as likely to die in childbirth than white women,[8] impacting the family structures of many marginalised families before they have had the chance to begin.

In the UK, structural racism means that 46 per cent of BAME children live in poverty, compared to just 26 per cent of children in white British families.[9]

Racism most certainly touches the lives of non-white people from its very earliest moments.

Sophie Williams

MY CHILDREN ARE TOO YOUNG TO UNDERSTAND

Children start learning about race from a surprisingly young age. When there is no conversation about the topic at home, they are left to form their own thoughts around it – whether via TV, friends or wider society – which if left unchallenged or discussed turn into beliefs and biases by the time they reach adulthood.

From three months old, babies are more drawn to faces that match the race of their parents or caregivers.[10]

From the age of two and a half, children begin to use race as a factor in deciding who to play with.[11]

Between four and five years old, learned racism is at its peak in children. Though by the time they reach five years old Black and Latinx children don't show a preference towards their own racial groups, white children do, showing strong biases in favour of whiteness, as well as having learned to associate some racial groups with a higher social standing than others.[12]

Whether we want to realise it or not, our children form these views from the societies they live in. When we don't discuss and challenge these views, we pave the way for the continuation of the same issues that we face today.

Sophie Williams

MY PARENTS ARE TOO OLD TO CHANGE

Older people do not get a free pass to perpetuate racism, even if their beliefs are deeply rooted and long held.

Marginalised people never get too old to be discriminated against.

Take time to explain your point of view to older people in your family and community. Use opportunities across the media that you consume and use the news cycle to start conversations that you may not have had before.

If these are new conversations, the people you are talking to may not even be aware that your beliefs are any different to their own, or how important this is to you.

Change isn't immediate, it can be long and frustrating, but every one of us has our actions impacted by our beliefs, and those actions go on to influence the society that we live in.

Most of us are not exactly the same person we were five or ten years ago – I know I'm not even the same person I was a month ago.

You have learned and grown as a person in your life, and others can do the same, it's just about finding the best way to reach them.

Everyone matters, regardless of how old or young they are.

Sophie Williams

TALK TO EXISTING LEADERS

Start with a mental audit of the additional communities that you're a part of.

Consider how diverse these organisations are, and what their leadership demographics look like. Are they representative of the racial breakdown of society as a whole? If not, it's time to examine the structural reason that may be preventing equal access for everyone.

If the communities that you're a part of are not representing society, you can start by simply addressing that with those who are in positions of power within them. Ask if they have noticed the inequity, and if so what they are doing to address it.

You can offer to support them in their efforts, or even take ownership of areas where your skills lie, to push for change more easily and effectively.

Sophie Williams

BECOME A LEADER

If leaders in your community are not willing to address racism or inequity, consider if you or someone you know can challenge their position, particularly if it's an elected role with a fixed term.

Just as we can impact the shape of politics by running for seats in elected office, we can impact the smaller communities that we're part of.

It may also be possible to make internal subgroups to ensure that anti-racism remains on the agenda, and the work that is needed is able to happen.

Sophie Williams

LOBBY LAW— MAKERS

The democratic process can seem impossibly far away, too far away to touch or influence. I promise you that is not the case.

We live in a representative democracy. Elected officials are voted in by you and me to represent and serve the needs of their constituents.

There are a lot of ways to engage in tackling racial, social and educational inequality in your community. You can do this by reaching out to your Member of Parliament or local councillors, by:

Writing letters and emails;

Attending Member of Parliament surgery hours;

Making email templates for others who are time-crunched

10.
BECOME AN ECONOMIC ALLY

Every time we make a purchase, click on an ad, share a link with a friend, we are supporting businesses.

Where and how we spend our money can have far-reaching consequences both for those businesses that we support, and the ones we overlook.

It is up to us to support the brands that we want to thrive and exist in the future, and to move away from those that we don't believe in.

Sophie Williams

DEMAND MORE FROM BRANDS

If a brand you like made a statement and then failed to make change, reach out to them. Publically and privately. Ask them why. Remind them that their statement of solidarity wasn't an act in itself, but a promise of an act that has failed to materialise.

Making change can be challenging, and if brands think they can avoid doing it, they will. Many brands engaged in performative allyship in 2020, putting out statements crafted by PR teams without any intention of doing the work or making any real changes.

Pay close attention to the businesses to which you give your money. Do they align with your beliefs? Did they continue to push anti-racism when the news cycle moved on?

How do they treat their workers? What is the make-up of their board of directors like, is it a diverse range of people?

Just as our body language needs to match our words and beliefs, so should that of the brands that we support with our money and patronage.

Apply pressure, ask questions and keep them accountable for making the change that we need to see.

Sophie Williams

TALK WITH YOUR MONEY

Your spending power matters. A lot.

Most businesses are, first and foremost, profit-driving enterprises.

In order to continue to push profits, businesses need to be aligned with, or at least not alienate, the majority of their customer base.

Boycotting brands can have serious impacts on their bottom line, and can force them into making changes that they otherwise might not have.

When we work together to funnel our money into brands and organisations that are doing the work, and to take it away from those who aren't willing to engage in meaningful or tangible ways, we can be significant forces for change.

Spending money is an endorsement – not just of a product, but of the people who benefit from your money and their values.

Be mindful of who you are giving your hard-earned money to, what they stand for, what they will do with it and what message that sends about the issues that matter most to you.

Sophie Williams

BUY
BLACK

If we're looking for brands that don't uphold white supremacy, brands that are founded and run by marginalised people are a great place to start.

Black-owned businesses are twice as likely to be rejected for loans which are essential in the early stages of most new companies, and so from their very earliest days, they are at a financial disadvantage.[13]

When we buy from marginalised communities, we help to put money back into those communities, returning the power and resources to those who need it the most.

Sophie Williams

MAKE DONATIONS

Donating to charities and organisations that are in line with your beliefs or that provide direct assistance to those you want to help is a really impactful way to be part of making change.

On a day-to-day basis, setting up a standing order or direct debit to a charity doing work you believe in helps giving monetary support become an act of habit.

In moments of crisis, if you're able, it's great to seek out organisations who are doing the active work, and to look for ways to support them, or to share their message with those who may be able to do so.

Always research organisations before donating so you can be confident your money is being used in a way that is in line with your values and beliefs.

11.
KEEP UP THE MOMENTUM

Allyship is not a one and done thing, it's a long process of working, accepting setbacks and keeping on keeping on.

One key to making sure this really is a movement and not a moment is to find ways to stay motivated, and to turn one-time actions into easily repeatable habits.

Marginalised people are tired, our fight has been long, hard and largely thankless.

After decades and generations of fighting for basic human rights and equality, and being denied them at every turn, many of us are burned out, overwhelmed, and yet we have to continue to push every day.

The resilience, passion and drive can be hard for anyone to maintain in the face of feelings of fear, helplessness and fatigue.

An important part of an effective anti-racist ally's role is keeping these movements and discussions progressing and at the top of the mind in the world and in their own communities.

Sophie Williams

THIS IS A MARATHON, NOT A SPRINT

It's been said so many times that it's a cliche, but it's absolutely true.

This is a long-term commitment, and for many people, small, regular actions are going to be more sustainable than huge bursts of energy that burn brightly but quickly fizzle out.

Set calendar reminders to check in with yourself and take stock of the things you've done to see how far you've come.

Make a time-based action plan and try to stick to it.

Grab a group of friends and make accountability check-ins.

Don't be frustrated when change is slow. It doesn't mean nothing is happening, it just means we need to keep applying the pressure to make the world the one that we want to live in.

Stay well, stay focused, stay active.

Sophie Williams

FIND WAYS TO MAKE REGULAR CONTRIBU- TIONS

Making a donation is a great and valuable thing to do, and if a one-time donation is all you can afford, it's still going to do a lot of good.

But if you're able to find ways to make donating a more regular part of your allyship practice, that's even better.

Research organisations that are doing work that speaks to you the most, and look at the ways in which they ask for support. It might be that you can set up a direct debit, or a standing order.

Talk to your employer to see if donations can be taken out of your monthly or weekly salary before it gets to you, so that the charity benefits from the pre-tax amount, and you don't have to see it come in and go back out.

It's also possible that your employer can match charitable donations to some organisations. Investigate what you can do to make your money go further.

Sophie Williams

MAKE SPACE FOR MESSY FEELINGS

Conversations around race and racial injustice can churn up a lot of messy feelings, for everyone.

Whether it's the feelings that you experience as you educate yourself further in your allyship about injustice, or the feelings that allyship work brings up in other people, activism is an emotional space.

Make space for those messy feelings in yourself and others.

Feeling confused or uncomfortable doesn't mean you should stop, it means it's challenging and you're playing your part in making a change.

BE PREPARED TO REPEAT YOURSELF.

A LOT

As frustrating as arguments from people who want to fight to maintain the status quo of white supremacy are, they're rarely original or imaginative.

You can save yourself time, energy and frustration by formulating stock responses to comments like 'All lives matter', or 'But what about Black on Black crime, and abortions too!' which can help to avoid burnout.

Sophie Williams

CREATE REGULAR CHECK-INS

Every week on my @OfficialMillennialBlack Instagram account I ask people what they have done in the last seven days to continue their anti-racist allyship work, and every week I hold my breath, terrified that no one will reply.

I'm always relieved as the responses come in, but I can't deny, there are fewer now than there used to be.

Create check-ins for yourself and your community. Hearing what other people have done can be a great source of inspiration, and knowing that you're going to be asked what you've done can give us the nudge we need to stay active.

You can also use this as an opportunity to share the things you've learned.

Share links, articles, books and pages that you have found useful with your friends and community.

Not only is this a great opportunity to engage new people and spread the message, it can open up conversations that can deepen and further your activism.

Sophie Williams

CELEBRATE SMALL WINS

Celebrating small wins is essential, and probably the best way to stay motivated and on track.

Don't wait for a law to pass before celebrating progress.

Big changes are made up of a whole series of smaller wins.

Notice them. Celebrate them. Feel pride in your achievments. Push for more.

Sophie Williams

DON'T FEEL THAT YOU'VE DONE YOUR PART

When change is slow and fights are hard, do not give up. This is when we need allies most of all.

Do not think you've done your part, and now someone else can come up behind you and take the baton. That is not how this works.

The opportunity to drop out of this fight is a privilege. Don't take it.

FURTHER READING

It's important to keep learning, growing and challenging yourself. Here are some reading recommendations to get you started:

- *Me and White Supremacy* – Layla Saad
- *Why I'm No Longer Talking to White People about Race* – Reni Eddo-Lodge
- *Freedom Is a Constant Struggle* – Angela Davis
- *Between the World and Me* – Ta-Nehisi Coates
- *They Can't Kill Us All* – Wesley Lowery
- *Natives* – Akala
- *How to Argue with a Racist* – Adam Rutherford
- *Waking up White* – Debby Irving
- *How To Be an Antiracist* – Ibram X. Kendi
- *So You Want To Talk About Race* – Ijeoma Oluo
- *Brit(ish)* – Afua Hirsch
- *The Good Immigrant* – Nikesh Shukla
- *White Fragility* – Robin DiAngelo
- *Black and British* – David Olusoga
- *The Power of Privilege* – June Sarpong

Resources for children and young people:

- The Conscious Kid – Instagram account
- A Mighty Girl (www.amightygirl.com) – a directory of books with non-white lead characters, broken down by age range
- *Antiracist baby* – Ibram X. Kendi
- *This Book is Anti-Racist* – Tiffany Jewell
- *Anti-Racism Starts With Me* – Kadeesha Bryant

ENDNOTES

1   'Black people "40 times more likely" to be stopped and searched in UK', *Guardian*, 4 May 2019

2   Pay Equity and Discrimination, Employment, Education and Economic Change, Institute for Women's Policy Research

3   Women and the lifetime Wage Gap: How many woman years does it take to equal 40 man years?, National Women's Law Center fact sheet, May 2019

4   Race inequality in the workforce, Georgina Bowyer and Morag Henderson, Carnegie Trust UK, 2020

5   Workers of color are far more likely to be paid poverty-level wages than white workers, Economic Policy Institute, June 2018

6   Black Boys Viewed as Older, Less Innocent Than Whites, Research Finds, American Psychological Association, 2014

7   'The British school-to-prison pipeline', Karen Graham in *Blackness in Britain* (eds) Kehinde Andrews, Lisa Amanda Palmer, Taylor and Francis, April 2016

8   Saving Lives, Improving Mothers' Care, MBRRACE UK Maternal Report, November 2018

9   Child Poverty Action Group Facts and Figures, July 2020

10   'Three-month-olds, but not newborns, prefer own-race faces', Kelly et al in *Developmental Science* 8(6):F31–6, Wiley, December 2005

11   'Do infants show social preferences for people differing in race?', Kinzler and Spelke in *Cognition* 119(1):1–9, February 2011

12   'A Social-Cognitive Developmental Theory of Prejudice', Frances E. Aboud in *The Handbook of Race, Racism and the Developing Child* (eds) Stephen M. Quintana and Clark McKown, January 2012

13   'Black-owned firms are twice as likely to be rejected for loans. Is this discrimination?', *Guardian*, 16 January 2020